Idle Winds Of The Flask

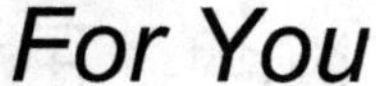
For You

Table of Contents

The Trickster Only Fools Himself

Chesapeake

ii

T

Completion, Destined And Doomed To Start Again

Aeven

At the time you materialized there was a blast -
colors transmuted to vivid tones exposing the strings
of reality - all of which were affixed to you
all sounds in the vicinity gravitated towards you and
as they passed by, told me your name
laws that had been known turned fallacy in this
moment
the sun had lived just to expose your beauty to him
every day and the moon to cast her jealous light upon
you at night
the grip of madness, the plagues of generations, the
iniquity of history, the brutish wars, the desolation of
culture, the lack of compassion; the balance of good
and evil, right and wrong, love and hate

-it all came to stop. All that remained was a figure
that Venus would idol and my want for you

A Candle Held For You

It is for you whom a rainbow shows
Your magnificence hence a daffodil grows
A decadence enhanced by incandescence
Diaphanous skin gleaming same shade as full moon
Whole is the soul glittering about, lacking holes and scars
Eyes which were the objects inspired the stars
Lips a salty sultry red left jaundiced Mars
Satin spider-woven locks envied by all
Every art spills pale compared to your view
Captivation comely left Avarice speechless

Ciel

the linen of the sky embedded with gold starlight. too
bright to gaze but not enough to wonder.
illumination made from perfection shrouds my eyes
brilliance.
when the infinite blaze reveals itself the earth vocalizes
back.
with true essence it leaves the observer blind, with
true power it leaves an imprint.
it is not confined with communication from visual
divinity, when sharing a bond with the ultimate fire it
vibrates violently to acknowledge the tether of
existence.
the ancient one stares directly through you into your
soul with its ability to flood all through its unrelenting
presence.

To The One Who Provides Answers

each eternal minute everlasting would dare not be a
sufficient amount of time with you
Prometheus will fight to take his fire back with which
I use it for my last sight to watch your eyes meet mine
my soul claimed to have met you once before
my heart agreed
my mind not comprehending but went forth
all that lay before a desolate and disparaging
nightmare
all that befalls to be heavenly since you have graced
my presence
an imprint unmistakable, as God tears up for giving
the apple to one as beautiful and immaculate as you
I was longing for the opportunity, my journey all just
to get to you
breaths not worth taking until the air I tasted was
yours
participation in a forgotten and forsaken world
unbearable till you accompany this broken stone

I shall perform the rest of the end in subservience to
the one who gave life its originality, whom all this
was for
My equal
My soul
Myself
the lingering semblance will attest to this passion
returning till infinity becomes apathetic towards itself
and tires of the repeating archetypal séance

Move Your (Flase) Body

Erase the boundaries of flesh
Indulge in the energy that comprises you, there are no restraints
A force blows through, the bass a hypnotic bump
guiding light feet to adjust to its presence
Treble clears the mind and soothes the soul, worry
melts like a lingering iceberg, a height now sunk
Spirits of old attach and mend to cleanse a faulty and disconnected psyche
Sparse are moments such where death, love, and life
entwine yielding the yearn of the ultimate
In this form, the goblet of omnipotence is held
The dunce is the king
The miscreants are royalty
The plebeians now aristocrats, advocating for once
their own and final expression
Equality and kinship among dance

Wish

Humankind
Men and women alike long to satiate an appetite
concerning pleasure, devour desire
Addition of religion which makes taboo natural
primal urges enhances the untouchable, unattainable
to ooze more juice from forbidden and tantalizing
fruit
Whether he to she, she to he, he to he, she to she, she
and she and he, he and he and she, they and them, so
on and so forth
A man's wife may not be coveted by decree but if she
does not get what she deserves, then that say is
reversed
A woman's husband sometimes needs an extra push
after a hard days work
Contact begins before its permissible
A catch of the eyes, a glimpse of glistening skin, a
drape of flowing hair dripping vanilla scent

Accidents do occur and a bump into a beautiful stranger may never feel better at least until vocal seductions are spoken
In tender exchanges perception enhanced, a simple rub of the skin excites and keeps us coming back for more
A pair of cherry lips, many can attest, taste as sweet as they look and as soft as well and from there tensions and frustrations only rise to be discharged
Unspoken acts performed, stroked with bliss, caressed limbs, smooth tones, palpated attraction ensured and shared, hands clasp linen, eyes roll ecstasy, body trembles, heart pulsates, abdomen tightens, legs quiver, feet relax, toes entwine, and the essence of the exquisite explodes left exhaustive but rejuvenates till eros meets eroticism once more
Don't deny yourself
Hedonism and debauchery are the only worth of a tormented and torturous world
Pain only makes pleasure feel so much better

To worship an ideal form, a godly being, can be done here with the gifts of lust and passion

Omniscience

Our words never seemed to meet naturally
A sign that compatibility never managed to
materialize
Utterances never felt, just departed
I want to just experience feeling
No filtering, no translations
Emotional raw exchanges
Words tell too well what innately remains obscure
Causeries constituted of charm, never distress, never
harsh tones, nothing of substance, no thought present
Lamentably, contemporary relational structure's sole
foundation being fantasy, characters whose purpose is
to please or flesh a fictitious role

B

A sorrowful sleep endured when I became
A trance transfixed upon untouchable skin
A letter never to be read, only touched by tears
A thousand and one dusks sat confined stationary
A million thoughts connecting
A brake too weak to stop myself
A heart too big to sink indifference
A plan to fall short
A wish that meeting never parts
A brilliance dazzling your eyes once again
A promise meant to be heard, not kept
A run never ceased
A chase never caught
A fire never out
A cloud ever floating
A ruse ever played
A road ever endless
A song ever sung

Fashion

Resembling your broken face
I wanted to depart, but no movement would assist
Ice foretold me of this event in reflections
Something I never knew
About myself
I watched the rise and fall of the king's light
You yelled in that moment
To me
To anything listening
A trance tough to terminate
Fabrications of that magnitude
Formed from deceitful revenants
Or
Assistant angelics
Of that
I was once more left unsure
Trivial, passing of time
Fruitless, a pursuit of any
Meaningless, days to writhe

The warmth you used to provide
The smiles you used to greet
The colors you used to evoke
An artisan of life, a philosopher of death, a mother to seeds, a teacher to dregs

Yes, indeed the yell of yours reached me
Only because
I was in the same place it was
A vacuum timeless, not rooted in absolute
A loop only the faithless witness
A spot ingrained upon a damaged mind
A sea shrouded senseless
Scream inescapable

I'm still there
Trying to get to you
Before you leave me
Once again

Sacrilege

Till that day
I will wait for you
Even if you never come

Haze

Sometimes
Morning lights along amnesia, the blow of night before reduced
Sometimes
Morning intrusive brings regret, telling of your failures and fears
Just like yesterday

What Could Have Been

Fitting the observer's chair, accompanying the
passenger's seat
I watched my desire unfold before my eyes
no thought, just motion
couldn't control it
too late

Blank

at what cost does your life start to have meaning
is it a measly paper currency
is it 100 dollars
10000 rubles
1000000 yen
is it a digital number
of likes
of value
having a company
selling your soul
working your mind away
obtaining a degree
that puts you in debt and pits you against your peers
for a wage lower than decades prior
is it finding that old feeling
is it smoking
drinking
chasing the dragon
is it blood laid on a battlefield of oil

is it scars
is it a donation plate in church
is it the struggle
the release from boredom
the trauma you went through and must overcome
your mortgage finally paid off
your grandson's graduation
a job that pays
 well for sitting around
is it knowledge
 of meaningless events
 of what financial institutions make you
 believe
 of yourself
is it having a family
 a child you secretly loathe
 a father that won't share his wealth
 a spouse that only cheats occasionally
is it the american dream
 coming from another country, only to learn
 they're all the same oppressive dictatorship
your love for another

your love for yourself
your hatred for yourself
your hatred for the one you once loved
 it's just easier to stay with them
is it criminal activity
 an urge to go against all
is it your duty as an outstanding officer
 to police the nation ruled and abused by   industry
 a standard opposing real freedom and
individuality
 to feel above a broken system
what about life? nature?
do you enjoy the scenery
the greens and blues and browns
it all meshes wonderfully, does it not?
is it the big city
coming from a small flyover town
carrying out your dream to be something, someone
is it to matter
is it to be adored
is it to be normal
is it to be loved

is it to destroy
is it to be feared
is it to be powerful
is it to be hated
is it to find out
 why we're here
 what we're doing
 where we're from
 where we're going
 what it all   means
is it for others
or yourself
for some it's okay
for some it's hell
I hope your life means
something   to you

Lone

The air stopped moving
The lights went out
All known before ceased
I fell into myself, just like before
Time reserved for those still pulsing
Logic collapsed
Movement withdrawn
Motionless abandon
The heart regained its pattern
Awoken from call
Bound duty resided
Comrades who've experienced
Death-loss-anguish-failure-defeat
Pulled me out of the sandy grave
Reunited with the deathly date
In the moment, none sensed sense
But I heard who was calling
Telling me maybe
It was time to go home

If I made it back

Box

Terrible tinctures strewn
Mold maunders mellow
Stench putrid, excremental loiter
Four walls never seemed so close
Unrecognized substances, once taking edible form
shared porcelain landings with roaches accepting of
their neighbors
Lines, needles, bongs, tabs, pills
Dim, lights not dare shine lest disgust be disregarded
as before
Former puffy dusty blankets colored tri - protect the
roomers from the gospel that is time, though at
certain times a halo like silhouette is adorned, the
cracks of light exposing air particulate
An outmoded corduroy sofa scarred tears and burns
exhales aroma, cigarettes lit once too long
Cries muffled in a distant room
The breathless attempting to breathe
Location: nadir

Omnipotence

A new god has emerged
The commons observe a handheld preacher
Our lord cries for our attention, and we obey, during
the most crucial of times
Behind the wheel
During the prosecution
Serving the atonement
The Technocratic One
Always watching
Always listening
Always tracking
Always selling
Relieve your boredom
And contractually carry your savior
We can count on the holy father and mother to raise
our young
As they navigate through the harsh upbringing of the
blue-light spillway

Prisoner Of The Unknown/Idle War

Acquired you have, the wealth of to know
Above the hands, in the face protrudes the glow
Devil's arithmetic allows the flow
Guised as help, a hypnotic trance
The jig of oblivion, our song and dance
Follow the institutions for finance
In the midst of the big and small
Even the innocent to it shall fall
Think quick, too late, ensnared are we all

As you and I have seen a degradation of everything
A mockery of the old ways
I wish and hope for better days
A time when those will look up from the silicone
grasp
And understand why time has passed
A rapid pace, this is no doubt
The problem humanity cannot figure out
While it stares them in the eyes

It leaves us blind and sanitized
Yet may be truth that we seek
But faux truth that is left to wreak
By habit alone what we have done
We allowed to replace the image of the Sun
Trading the warm real illumination for soft deceitful virtual luminosity

Operator

Indifferent objects and ignorant faces cast

lifeless limbs and failing hymns

a distant memory of a dead dream

One Culture Under Corporations

locked behind ironic bars
seclusion in apathy
generations cursed by predecessors
enemies for neighbors
the me, theme is me
values vanished
good guys are neutral at best
social media, the controlled freedom, the mask of modernity
sedated drivers
uninspired artists
assassination apparelled assistance
arguments over empty space
virtual war over imaginary domain
flock of sheep, media the herder
pied piper lulling
opinion generated
thoughts bought for free
reasonable is unreasonable

wrong portrayed right
patriotic terrorism
identities sold
fashionable abomination
this was my home

Ubiquitous

Your ignorance protrudes once more
Speaking on loyalty as a universal mandate
Such recompense a curse worthy of fools
This world led by indifference, existentialism, and post-irony
This culture cultivated by inorganic mega-monolithic demigod corporations and institutions
Plan for nothing sacred as poor lies crash to the floor, espoused from rich lips
The concept of fealty remains null in this state of dividends
What you think you own, can always be stolen
What you think you see, has always been careful illusion
Who you think you are, you were born broken
The words you hold affiliation, invented with binding intention
Pray you make it to see through mass delusion that most are so fond of wearing

Your All

Keep it
Keep your grades
Keep your marks
Keep your mistakes
Keep your choices
Keep your stubbornness
Keep your foolishness
Keep your false hope
Keep your jaded heart
Keep your washed mind
Keep your lack of belief
Keep your nose high
Keep your vanity
Keep your materials
Keep your money
Keep your logo belt
Keep your diamond encrusted watch
Keep your head-concealing hat
Keep your light blockers

Keep your once-a-year shoes
Keep your obnoxious car
Keep your Manatee removing vessel
Keep your flying contraption
Keep your home 20 rooms too many
Keep your sullen women
Keep your arrogant men
Keep your gang affiliation
Keep your legal gang affiliation
Keep your politicians
Keep your government
Keep your murderous food
Keep your tainted water
Keep your quick meals
Keep your infectious drugs
Keep your prescribed drugs
Keep your mass media
Keep your phony system
Keep your false God
Keep your ashen hands
Keep your quoted lies
Keep your narratives

Keep your span-reducing tech
Keep your knowledge
Keep your medical procedures
Keep your American Dream
Keep your flights to space
Keep your social media
Keep your escapes
Keep your uneducated families
Keep your dying brothers
Keep your prostituted sisters
Keep your suffering
Keep your conceit
Keep your drama
Keep your guns
Keep your knives
Keep your chemicals
Keep your urges
Keep your sanity
Keep it all   far away from me

Take Your Time

Hoarders hostage borders, flies tread skies
Keepers lurk deeper, liars keep not higher
Apprentice do dance for a master
Insult absorbed for chance to live faster
Guardians foretell omens they can dismay
Watch atop their fortress preventable decay
A license to kill is a license to sell
Common market but a wish in a well
The degrees of degrees, amount untold
A fold or flap, required only gold
The finest material - independence, only the wealthy hold
Is a house a home when owned by a bank?
Is a man a man when occupation is rank?
When the cost of death is free and the price of life exceeds it is up to man to bring inequality to its knees

The Murderer In Abbot Sane

Abbot Sane
Normal man
Some money
Some plan
One job
One love
One child
One land
One day
One zeroed
Up downed
Wife weaves
Tragedy strikes
No job
No love
No child
No land
No day
All lost

Hope gone
Satisfaction disband
What one
May do
When all
Has died
Nothing left
Not even
Tears formed
In cries
While others
March on
Living through
Better lives
Abbot Sane
Crawls back
Avoiding his
Makers eyes
Torment grief
Far over
The edge
Abbot Sane

Falls under
Far under
Deep under
No mortal
Dare go
Gave soul
Bid adieu
And departed
This cold
Rigid world

This One's For The Stricken

There are no stories sung for the ages about the losers
The ones who bare the accolade of suffering
Those who die without a name
Those whose only experiences are misfortune and pain
The black sheep
The overshadowed
The footstep follower
The career crushing injured athlete
The solitary
The broken
The unique
Those rejecting limited advancement
Those socratic learners who simply ask why
The horrors not highlighted by the news
The child taken by the stray bullet
The child starved by caretakers and protectors with better to do

The parents whose marriage is torn from a child never to be held
The child murdered and raped for no reason aside this being their path
There are no redemption arcs
Those to be stepped on, dished out, abused, mistreated, used, forsaken, smitten, diagnosed, branded, marked, isolated, damaged
It is from these few hurt that they fade among the true dead who know no conflict
Only the suffocated may fight to breathe for life
Laws in place to feed the interests of a few, not to help the many
The better man should not lose because a leader fabricates an infraction
What do you do when injustice is the only legal form of justice

Watch The Air Traveler

Truth cannot lie upon sullied ground
Buried in unfamiliar ways,
Ancient ways, mouthed by ancient tongues,
tarnished by tyrants whose experiment drags on
Highlighted names, be wary, hold connections to
groups who serve misery
No man my god
No god my master
No life my own
Founded on false pages, idols, saints
Imprinted youth, ignorant are the old
If you alone, find proud to be
If answers seek, observe silently
Truth lays sleeping on distant greens where the
reaches of cult are not whispered, awaiting for the
brightest of days to beckon once more

I dislike format,

confined to a rhyme   we need vision

obscurity
imagination

placed upon

crush the constraints
by ourselves

implanted

and
others

the

game

manipulated

boundless

makers

limited

you
are
you
while
their
rule
their

limitless

Think

Once voyaged atop rock
When I came across sand
Dead stone crumbled to dust
No life sewn among land
In the distance a sea
Filled with gold, silver bones
Fluid drains from the sky
A setting of unknowns
Welkin dormant in green
Fluttering creatures wing
Sight not believed suffice
Least not human being
Ra's splendor, chroma red
Radiance confounded
First light to bestow nip
Slight dimness surrounded
One satellite? No three
Reflect infinity
From moons sight: future, past

Pure lucid clarity
Stars drift sporadically
Spelling out night and day
Here no time resolute
Celestial highway
Never want for leaving
This empyrean place
Remains for you to see
In both close and far space

The love of the world

Quaint queries of a breeze, its question a nudge
Fascinating fixation of a crowd, exaltation expressed through exhale
Magnificent meadow, a series of raised figures whose islands lend green hands
Coarse cumulus, popcorn and cotton candy laid out upon an endless dish of blue

Serendipitous Sunday, sounding it's seductive sultry sonics and harmonics heavenly had for the piquant populace potpourri hosted harmoniously by the most gratuitous gracefully glorifiable mother whose mounds made for molding and multiplying, she give to the - her offspring, sons and lords, daughters and ladies, flora and fauna, blessed are those who be notified of and nourished and nestled by her fertile boundless body.

Well Deserved

this is not just a poem
confined to a piece of parchment
or a text strewn upon digital canvas
the plight of a few
not afraid to express themselves
a story of the intertwined, fantasy and reality
the two meet upon the diagram
where current flows and hands keep up
freeflow form, the connection between mind and sublime
it doesn't have to be learned or taught, unlike instruments
a natural linguistic expression
the individual holding its own marker
penning the events or lack of
desires, hopes, dreams, distresses
all with the intention of reaching an audience
in the hopes that maybe
at least someone else, feels the way they do

Read Me

hey you
yeah you
not symbolic you, not metaphorical, not rhetorical
you
the one who reads these words
these words are alive not by just the author
or chance, they share sentience as you and I
they are cosmic, only interpreted by the author in
order to communicate to you because you wrote them
as well
you had to see these words because simply if not this
would not be your life
it would be someone else's
by stumbling upon the written you acknowledge that
for some reason things aligned in order for you to be
here in your current state as you are
that these words breathe and reflect the same, they are
here for you. to be absorbed. you take them in. they
are your environment. you are your environment.

everything around you is you. a different form, coming from the one who designed it all which is also you.
I hope whatever you are going through ceases. I hope you stop putting yourself through torment. I hope you realize that love and hope lingers, even through a culture far removed from any legitimate understanding. I hope you realize that you define yourself. That you're not alone. That you are the most important thing in your life.
These words simply are not just from me, but from the world, the aether, the element holding us together, the membrane, what makes us separate in form but not origin; these words come to me in relation to you as they could not take part without you, the reader in relation because not only would I not be writing this but these words write themselves through me as all things do. We are ourselves and all around us, emotions are states of our world and everything holds consciousness. It is meant to be so. Don't worry about losing yourself, when this is over there are no borders between here and there, skin and

air. You will see as it was, what it will be, what it always is.

May you be comforted by your own presence, may the wind let it be known this is your land, let the sky tell you that your mind is of free reign, let your clothes not confine you to the earthly state.

Let yourself dismiss the boundaries and sink into the whole, melt and stick to soil to grow life or evaporate into the rain you wish to spread.

You must know, all things pass. The cosmic game will be over soon. For this, I will wait for you, the reader, to write me - these words - again until you figure out everything that you need to.

Let us part, I will be here. Always.

Six

Six sticks stuck static sat sickened by wood
What wood would wail with warped writhing limbs
Lay leisurely level let lean likened lazily loose and
lackadaisically left to brood
Born by blood, brought bound basic bondage to be
buried and burrowed to reemerge
Reimagined reanimated reborn rafting and rowing to
reach rest only to engage again
Existence also effervescence absolutely ever or never
allowing to ensure appropriation of a respawn
Choose to come back or dwell in a room of your own
in the sempiternal charade

Can't

Ruminating on rumors, rummaging through
Rorshack rubble
Once a foundation flourishing - finalized upon faulty
furnishings
Spectacle suspended, past scraping the sky, present
scantily spread
Crumbles and tumbles, concrete and timber,
corruption and trepidation
Sunsets set solemn, rainbows rouse rancor,
architecture assents annihilation
Silence befalls the broken, sound befuddles the barrier
between what should and should not be said

Along succeeding development may my next
structure solidify formidably

Carve Your Own

Count and countess of counting kept countenance though lacked accounting for cycling and recycling of the cycles faced in the cyclone of cyclical eras, errors and errs and heirs and flowing air of time teeming with temptation but temperamental all the same, so many sought supersedence along sovereignty and autonomy but the autonomous became synonymous with the monotonous and day dulled and dwindled down to night known notoriously for nocturnal notions and antics the people proposed preposterous presuppositions of acting accordingly and anchored on an elaborate idea to do what they please, as it should be

Modern

Metamorphosed Ooze
Submerged fluid
Emerged liquid
Formed solid
Grounded supine
Cumbersome locomotion
Roused fidgeting
Inculcated inefficacy
Fleshly misdirection
Solitary confusion
Uncomely malformations
Constant acceleration
Verified submission
Disassembled aches
Refined indolence
Decaying juncture
Grounded prostrate
Moribund manifestation

A flash
Beginning's end

Please Return

where amongst the animated do you lie recluse my
brothers, sisters?
disguised behind the designated?
oh my family, I've known you briefly, caught your
soft yet passionate chattering
studied your message through your methods
yet still, our encumbrance so voluminous holds
burden
of what may be has not yet been
let yourself be shared with the rest
so love may return, coincide dredged pain
place the pain among the people
so genuine can be held like old

Feed Your Wings

Clouds ever long lapsed casing pareidolia
Wounded cognoscente
When answers among, no inquiries abound
When all noises play, doubt discern singular sound
Craft cheap, copied, covert, copious, conceited
Concrete cordon cause concocted cognition
Community cursed colorblind cozened "certified"
vision
Insight condemned, mundane ubiquitous commend
Abstract deficiency during structured necessity
Definitions defy cleverness and creativity
Let not your soul be starved of ingenuity
Beyond the curtain of authority cloistered calamity
Just a siphon
Pretension upon entrance - cripple, undermine,
debilitate, incapacitate
Contemplate beyond, snatch limitless divine

Recognize

loose remains the bond that once attached heaven to earth
a time when love fell, twinkling down and enriching the land along its residents

Seconds

Loneliness: the friend that never leaves
Yet again here I stand,
Alone two feet weigh down the barren land,
Not even sky stay immune to this tune,
It retires, collapses and crumbles to dune,
sea and earth although they may meet,
asunder and plunder another till defeat,
a young man loves, an old man dies,
a young woman cheats, an old widow cries

Have you heard the saddest story; of the Sun?
Banished he was to light, that one,
always affixed to his morning realm,
cursed he surmised with his shining helm,
but from day to eve he may glare a glimpse,
blushing lady of dark who nightly primps,
her confine among those that twinkle small,
prominence is hers about the great dark wall,
so gracious her beauty though it may be,

cursed to hide face quarterly,
opportunity amiss as years go by,
luminaries with own domain of sky,
wishing, hoping, waiting,
sitting, thinking, praying,
that one cycle they may share each other,
light in light illuminate the entire together,
eliminate the difference of dark and light,
turn night into day and day into night

Day

Where to dream drift?
Beyond comprehension
Here, answer untold
Lies sleep past stars
Underneath dormant
Carried along Styx
Each boat its own
Leaving calm
Enters bliss
During journeys great,
or mellow or fright
Lulled entrance
Gentle, light
Higher connection
Areas unmatched
Cataclysmic unfolds to lovers and family passed
So many places I wish I could stay

Only to wake into a perverse, harsh, unnerving
sensory factory

A beautiful World

Signal the horns
The time is brought
Used to be bought
What comes ahead?
Revitalization
Invigoration
Old forms new once more
Breath never taught to breathe
Pillars unseen now stand
Benefactors of all land
Sky breaks
Earth cracks
Ocean cries
Her azure hue touches all including ones above
Reformation
Truth of renaissance
We go back
To what was stolen
What was lost

Look

Fearful for the sanity that never was
Clinging to the option that ceased before starting
Pestering of old mind
Ignorant of old heart
Pestilence, a downfall of the stubborn
Non-existent, the fear behind fear
New fallacies to blame
Modern modes of religion blind our newly class of blighted
Fear, just the inconvenience to adapt to new belief, or truth
Claw for the chance to succumb to slavery
Fret for the freedom to overcome oppression
Looking in the wrong direction when the false is labeled truth
Nothing is a tie when it can be cut

What's done when handed the forged map,
coordinated from the womb?

No Walls

Cast aside rational
Escape to birth
Let foundation crumble
Exhume dead inside
Conscious fade,
Lined light
Duplicit façade,
Formless night
Combination of the wake, departed
Matrimony by the essence, discarded
Break free from frame
Blame sea sans shame
Bury lies, lay lame
Sickness within,
withdraw sin
Give it to your filthy autocratic god

Sense

there remains limitation of language
opt to rid yourself of barriers placed upon by speech
an invention of man will always be his downfall
in the last line alone the common phrase has been
popularized to man, and not the term people
rest not on the shoulders of giants when you have still
your own to flare
when you speak the word kiss, do you feel the touch
of another's lips to your own?
when you hear of love, do the weights on your heart
release?
when death is mentioned, do you recognize infinite
expanse and fragility of life in current form?
when soul is termed, do you believe it or even more:
do you feel your own aching and longing to rid itself
of the mortal wound?
relieve the bondage of linguistics and embrace feeling,
speech through touch, love of yourself and others
through action

All Hearts Rejoice And Conjoin

Notes sprung among fabrics
Legionaries carry their fliers
Has one such as you been known to?
Empty hearts pervade plastic homes
Full lies endorse a fanatics romance
Did you remember that instance?
Coarse outlines resemble images of
A rough draft lacks fulfillment
Were the clowns gathered around?
Broken landscapes signified alternative
Her greed held his heart at gunpoint
All that belongs to one always ends possessed by another
At least, that's the way they say it goes
The charade abrupt, fell for you too?
Or did you pick the flowers in the absence of your imagined lover?

Absence

In those times a dawning of a new era glistened in the
soon surpassed distance
When sun shone bright enough to light up a
fortunate future
If they knew what was to come maybe they would
climb once formidable trees to his kingdom
The few knew and allowed elapse of elementary time,
once recess now recession along repugnance
What was to come?
When the sun was replaced it glistened beams of
hatred upon all acknowledged for allowance stolen
from truth's light
Its successor never quite fit its borders correctly

After

Greetings from the flesh bid aetherial adieu
Skin from muscle to bone to heart to mind to soul to
source
Transient transporter this figure is till depart
Now realigned with the ultimate, where no container
holds, bounds unbinded, energy flows free
Look to the non-existent previous manifestation of
mortal time, it lingers no where
how what why
No more
Feel the place once below and before, realize it was
and has been always will eternally now future forever
All it was, a test
All you are, a drip of a drop of a deity dream

Antique

Views of weathered visages show memories that
whisper a distant longing but a close feeling
Those with and those without -
A dream
A family
A lover
Inevitably the blessedness of the withs crumble to the
valley of withouts
On these mounds of flesh of face I have witnessed
whole lives in an instant, reflecting back on my own
I voyage my life as a repetition of theirs, the same
mistakes my fathers made as do I, the choices of my
own just influences of old, places I've brushed across
the remainder of what civilization left, thoughts not of
my own but channelings of the ancients and gods
I have been shown the experiences of many in one
man's trial, it simply repeats
I've seen man exposed for what he is, what it is
Not as a human

The definition restricts and confines
I've watched a fantastic being, one capable of feeling and emotion unparalleled on it's brightest day
I've stood in the umbra of a creature who knew not of what it was but what it was capable of
I've understood breathtaking events and gazed tragedies unkind
I've felt the breakdown of the paradox of existence alongside those who wish to know what and why
I know this being, it is familiar to you and me
I have seen the death and rebirth of this immortal and will come to know my own
This container is not yet full

Slapped

inebriation - satisfaction
make the commoners a bit more tolerable
make existence easier to manage
churn the monotony
spit out cohesion
from time to time a man must decide
and take a dive within himself
what else may life be about
aside from discovering the outside is in

Are You Afraid Of What Lies Above

Man, his own lord
Slave and master
Subjugates
Directs
Being gives its own form
The light takes shape of its corners
Like water
Contained
The man that makes his beast
The man that makes his saint
The man that makes his devil
The man that makes his god
Obstacles placed to deceive by self device
Every ache
Every hunger
Every desire
Effective façade
Penitentiary pensioned by poised persona
The thing frightened of itself

The creature knows what it is
Apprehensive to admit
Paradoxical perpetual paradigm
The creation which molds itself
What to do when it is all yours?
Yours alone.
Eternity
Infinity
Await you.

Out

I've never been much of a man who cares for anything
Whether the world burns or floats is none of my concern
Nothing really matters here
Just the way the sun shines on a lone traveler
All beneath is a sole lapidary morphing gem to be as bright or dim as one sees fit
The trail is landscaped and generated by the walker
Zero-sum game
What you feel is what you get
What we feel is extension
What they feel is perjury
The light bearer accompanied with rudimentary torch
Do all believe what is written down here?
Or is that your line to cross?

Edict Of The Deceased

Time, the presence which subsidizes all
Joining and relating events, people, locations
An essential part of the aether, after all these cells, this abode, this universe a membrane and when the microscopic flows so the macro follows
So simple it is to remember
So difficult it is to forget
An overbearing but weightless hand rests upon all our shoulders
Today, I journeyed to no where
Nothing would take my place
Not being occupied, the strings pulled my thoughts yet again to be reminded of...
A feeling no name ascribed, but to each being assigned
A young boy may feel his fade
If he knows time waits for no man,
Not because its indiscriminate,
But because it is and is not,

It is chosen
Do you not see the end?
Do you not see the beginning?
Do you feel yourself?
Feel your memories, no matter how far they are fresh
Feel your demise, no matter how far it does occur
The Waven Master, The Grand Keeper
The titles of one who stays for mortal comfort
But absent for the Gods

It Should Be Dry

Let the rain dampen these things
Let the silk of cloud allow my rest
I ask in this moment could it be again
Vicinities collapse, lands crack, but this rain will always pour
Lost feelings surface on rhythmical wet tapping daydreams
Heard is the somber rhymes that draw weak men in
Even hard minds relocate to absent shores
At end all who are desire and be lone
We cannot resist the thundering of time
Of flash, clap an instant, a weathered state of mind
Lead me o' windy captain to your heavenly storm
So I may reminisce, be reborn by drops of water once more

Displayed

Garden of life
Entwine
Dinner of deeds
Decline
A star falls
A curtain calls
A symphony folds
A dam holds
In and out
It's so
Round and round
Whirl flows
Side to side
The ride bides
Our repeating tides
Lives who've lied

Chaotic impracticality among organized remedy

From edge to edge it seems not rare, nor black nor white
The between is the current location
Great comparable to worse determined not the same situation
After all we stand on hallowed land, underneath a
sub-world lies unknown to above's observant eyes,
higher we may peer we wish to learn about up there
but alas we, the stones, caught in between the
nightmare and the dream, for it is in this space all
matters, manners, manuscripts, multitudes take place

Danny

Remain the great equalizer, shadow's dusky refuge creeps
Father of fear, teacher of congruency - all remains silent in the Dark
Where light resides it fixed follows lingering behind
The provenance of creation; primordial influence lay edging mistily on the horizon of forethought
Its origin never in reality but actuality, dormant in the mind of man turn monster
Do you feel the cull? The draw?
The apprehension? The power.
Antecedent to creation, derivation of sin
Its whisper enticing
Its caress subdued
Its desire chained
Sense pleasure that pleads to be set free
Carnal
Primal
Instinctual

Relinquish yourself
Allow Origin
Let it spread
Return to start

Defunct

Glassed shambles, fractured lines
Life's moratorium, ageless discrimination
So near the ones below
So high the ones above
Stay and see antics unmatched my long gone kin
I will be with you soon enough

Renounce

inhabitants of the other world
I implore you
show me your ways so I may not decay
here
the point blunted
the plot obscured
the premise transparent
there is no story here
nothing organic endures
the broadcasts poison and all seem to be contaminated
the breath of man, stenched through speech -
cowardice, indulgent, submissive, and noxious aroma
no us vs. them
it's only me vs. me
me vs. limbo
me vs. the final day
speed up
transition into present so I may know of a life worthy
of living

Play

Born below a blood moon, graveyard-covered night lay barren, no forms of light allowed to remain, no hanging their scintillating features among an oppressive black tarp. Since departure from void to vice not one moment passes magnetized dark force manipulating liminal boundaries of eye, arm, back, mind and all else inherited from nothing to thought to existence. Shackles of flesh align worldly forsaken paradigm abided by contracts which tethered soul enslaved continues attempting to catch angler god's never-ending ever-bright light. Peasants dream kings, kings dream gods, gods dream death, death dreams life. Return to be reborn, anew announced appropriately upon a plane ceaseless to motions forgone by this forgotten hollow, hovering a maw swallowing its own borders. The search not ends here, only a trite delay among the expanse of a being that knows not its own name nor origin.

Deception

this dwelling is an argument between soul mind body
the self as a god
the self as a spirit
the self as an animal
the self who knows all
the self who knows how
the self who knows now
the only battle waged between these forms

help

tired
of myself
of the stereotype i've created for myself
just to fit in your bubble
your idea of me
it doesn't exist
i pretended to be
to make you happy
to make your secure
to make you trust
to make you like me
this masquerade
dissolved
for me
long ago
i can't keep this appearance
anymore
what you felt, it was just an image
a persona

i just want someone to accept me for who i am
what i am
i desire only
to be real
to be true
to be free

Yes

In my world no laughter is echoed
No fire dances
No priests pray
No child has a father
No call is answered
No light lights
No wind glides
No cries are heard
No love labored
No dreams had
No birds sing
No mountains peak
No oceans wave
No rivers flow
No lakes contain
No sun shines
No clouds line
No grass greens
No table holds

No seat sits
No food tastes
No touch tells
No step walks
No ants crawl
No snow sticks
No ground stays
No windows reveal
No song sounds
No man feels
No woman cries
No drinks imbibe
No drugs do
No home houses
No crates carry
No weight weighs
No towel soaks
No carousel turns
No magic made
No eyes blink
No sleep slept
No one else

No god remains

Notes

the story is coming to a close
no more heroes
superman
isn't coming
to save
the day

The Fractal

A disorganized clutter parades as the divide amidst the wake and dream
The sub-layer of reality, what forms fantasy to subsist
Not mere speculation, the private world affects the public narrative
The current paradigm misapprehends any substantiation of such claims
But when not worshiping nor endowing the fundamentals of nature the sentient deteriorate into the hive mind of the mad
Balances must be checked within the realm but first within ourselves
The misty haze veiling this from that is shedding, wearing thin
Presently will the event occur in which the mass of collective man not tell spirit from self
The grip of the western culture warns introspection
It longs to be broken

Rest

A trace of a demon
Slithering
Crawling within the confines
Of where a soul took place
Oblivion's edge eclipses
Its source within
Black hole
Where order resided
Restrained by preordained notions
But when flowers wither
And oceans collide
The serpent will surge
And the world
And self
Will be devoured
Again
In the reclaimed age
Of Darkness

Set In Motion The Endless Tides

The beginning of the end starts to settle low in the atmosphere
Rasp dedicates itself to all manners of matter, present or absent from direct flow of what we know to be
From time to centuries a change is apparent to blow legislations down
The tides churn and beacon a new prized chariot
Poseidon must cycle, just as all do
The above has known to go below
In has been out, it's just out is in now
Sport your sports, don your corporate/governmental dons
The colosseum will slam its doors to the public once the audience wakes to find they and the warrior share the same field, not independent of the tamed and the entertained
Tempests brew, sun burns, Mandela effects us all in one way or another

What lurks underneath the primordial veil that
shadows the glass we stone upon?
Where lies the origin for origin or the end of the end?
May a story complete if its protagonist perdures no
change?
Are answers given freely or is freedom the wrong
answer?

Losing

What is reality?
What is a human?
Do you believe what you perceive?
Do you know who you are?
Were you present at your birth?
Is this a test?
Is this heaven?
Is this hell?
Is this purgatory?
Do all only witness their own?
Do you relish the words taught and what they spell?
Does the unnamed hold more value than the defined?
Do you wear the chains?
Do you pocket the keys?
Are absolutes available?
Does any of this matter?
Is this a dream?
Is this real?
Where does thought reside?

Are you lost?
Do you wish to be found?
What lies beyond?
Where is our father?
You think he really walks with you?
Do you detect the lies?
The lies others tell you.
The lies you tell yourself.
When felt inside do you feel the stir?
All feel and fear the storm.
Hold tight.

Seek

It's all been done before
All seconds already embedded in the grand catalog of time
Prior, present, post
The clock whose hand perpetual motion
Lives lived indefinitely
Deaths died and delayed dismally
Come back
Turn around
Hokie pokie, the jig of recurrence and reincarnation
Is anything so important when you know the end?
The answer antecedently innate and a mass aware
induces fugue sanctioning itself to carry on
It is death, death being life, life being rebirth
succumbing to the boundless zodiac wheel rotation of suffering and mortal recourse
Contemporaneously all-one, one-all
Living while dead, dead while alive
The solution within

Enigma of the being knowing itself and awareness
and its demise only to repeat the insipid trial till we
and the architect deem it concluded

All

Self
Mere collection of outside
Influence
Attribution to all
Surrounding
Lack of real
Barriers
Nothing truly rests
Alone
No such thing as
Separation
It is all just part of the
Singularity
Which one day I will
Return
Which one day you will
Return
Which one day we will
Return

Which one day will
Return

The Observer Didn't Know It Only Viewed Itself

to each man a meaning,
making his own maker,
attribution
escalation from each step
ascending to falling to zagging
observing self through manners inaccessible present
but wholly operable
a test provided itself
query without querent
race without finish
no beginning
no end
just

The Trickster Only Fools Himself

Somewhere God resides among his playground
happily ignoring wrongs to do what he can't in his
own space
His amnesia a gift self-wrapped so the unbearable
weight of being an author simultaneously written
itself may be extinguished, at least till the theater
resigns once more
A claimed, if not the only, reason for living is
curiosity and in the current iteration there is no such
thing
Everything solved, science says so
We don't tend farm or family when there are
supermarkets and digital comforts
All necessary interaction - pleasure, comfort,
connection, caring - half-heartedly and
inappropriately a tap or click away
The reluctant nihilist will soon wake from his self-
induced round of mishaps and engage in a boredom

shared with humanity this time in history bringing change
Only his whim this place beckons
Our prayers cannot be heard when the skies are closed
When the race horse dies you realize there never was a race, only was it claimed to be, a horse only knows to run
When the entertainment ends
When the show is over
When talking heads utter repetition
When music sounds only the same
When movies represent something greater than your own
May you lead us again
To a life worth living
Not a mouse chasing cheese
May you find your own peace
So you can rejoin the pieces of yourself you gave up just to find yourself piece by piece
Wasting my time
When you are always here
And always will be

Chesapeake

Sometimes I fall into oblivion
As I look above all I witness is fatality
I shed all that remains
Let me part the place that wrought me damned

ii

in subtle flickering sound of midnight the call of devils whispers trickle enticingly into my ears just like a warm kiss from the ethereal. not invitation but a re-welcome into descent of that which was buried but ever-present

T

I'M ALIVE
AND I CAN SEE MY MOUTH MOVE
BUT NOTHING WILL ESCAPE THIS TONGUE
THE ENDLESS TORMENT
OF A CEASELESS TORRENT
BETWEEN BITING A BULLET
AND CATCHING IT WITH MY HEAD
EVERYONE WILL MEET THEIR FATE
BUT NO ONE CARES
SCREAMING WITH THEIR MOUTHS CLOSED
DEFILING THE WEAK WITH THEIR EYES
GENERATIONS WHO NEVER FELT WARMTH
NO AMOUNT OF PERFUME COVERED THE
STENCH OF DECAY
THE FAMILY IS FAILING
THE SYSTEM WAS MADE TO FALL
ROLE PLAYERS PLAY MAKE BELIEVE
PRETEND THEY'RE SOMETHING
WHEN ALL WE ARE IS DUST AND DIRT

BITTERNESS STARTS TO TASTE SWEET
WHEN ALL IS BITTER
DOES ANY OF THIS MATTER
PEOPLE WALK AROUND CRUCIFIED
I MET GOD
HE TOLD ME I WAS HIM
HE HANDED ME THE STICK
AND LEFT ME HERE TO ROT
IT WAS A PARADISE
NOW IT'S AN ASYLUM
OUR SOULS ACHE
FROM THE POISON OF CONNECTION
MEMORIES LEAKING
LIKE CRANIAL FLUID
CAN A SOUL BE TAKEN FROM A MAN
ALL I SEE ARE THE DEAD
PRETENDING TO BE ALIVE
I MOVE BUT GO NOWHERE
I'M TRAPPED AND THERE'S NO ONE TO
CALL
INFESTED WITH APATHY
RIPPED FROM SLUMBER

TO BECOME REBORN
LET ME SLEEP
THE PEOPLE ARE DYING
THE ANIMALS RIP EACH OTHER APART
JUST TO STAY ALIVE
A CRUEL AND TWISTED WORLD
THE JESTER PARADES
THE KING FLAUNTS
TILL HE'S MADE THE PEASANT
WHEN HE IS TAKEN FROM THIS LIFE
I'M FLAGGING EVERYONE DOWN
BUT NO ONE SEES ME
THE STATE
OF IT ALL
IT'S HOPELESS
I'M ALL ALONE
I'M ALL ALONE
I'M ALL ALONE
I'm All Alone
I'm all alone
i'm all alone
im all alone

imallalone

Completion, Destined And Doomed To Start Again

to which all things come
the end
outside within
inside without
distinction denied between flesh and land
songs only heard by those who sing them
fatally emancipate lovers shackled by confines of this
fettered determinest outcrop
the light of a real day, part me here to seek
beyond morality's futility, surpass melodrama of the
unwavering children,
bar me from an existence not mine,
situated emptiness substituted for comfort, bar my
entrance here - the cursed promised land of guilt.
frivolity of the faithless grind, I've done this before
a place truly where you think and you are,
where freedom not a slogan but a building block

deny my consultation and force me myself, I must see what I am
longing for an unseen landscape, an area not here but
felt soft through a dampened sense
a sight escaped from soul
take me to the one to which I belong
because I know
I don't belong here

www.ingramcontent.com/pod-product-compliance
Lightning Source LLC
LaVergne TN
LVHW050316160826
845677LV00014B/3423

* 9 7 9 8 8 4 4 1 7 9 3 4 1 *